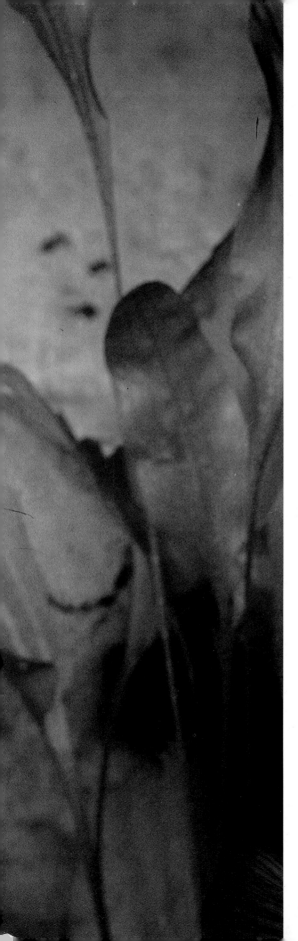

# Discus as a Hobby

by

**Jim E. Quarles**

**SAVE-OUR-PLANET**

**T.F.H. Publications, Inc.**
1 T.F.H. Plaza • Third & Union Aves. • Neptune, NJ 07753

## Contents

**Photography:** R. Annunziata, Aqualife, Dr. H. R. Axelrod, Bede Verlag, K. L. Chew, D. Cooley, P. Gallagher, D. Jordan, M. Junge, B. Kahl, Midori Shobo, F. Mori, H. Musstopf, M.C.&P. Piednoir, J. Quarles, H.-J. Richter, F. Rosenzweig, M. Tatematsu, D. Untergasser

# Dedication

I dedicate this book to my wife, Jane, whose understanding, love, and support has passed all bounds. She has suffered through all stages of discus fever with me over the past 30 years. I further dedicate it to all the wonderful discus who have graced my tanks.

Distributed in the UNITED STATES to the Pet Trade by T.F.H. Publications, Inc., One T.F.H. Plaza, Neptune City, NJ 07753; distributed in the UNITED STATES to the Bookstore and Library Trade by National Book Network, Inc. 4720 Boston Way, Lanham MD 20706; in CANADA to the Pet Trade by H & L Pet Supplies Inc., 27 Kingston Crescent, Kitchener, Ontario N2B 2T6; Rolf C. Hagen Ltd., 3225 Sartelon Street, Montreal 382 Quebec; in CANADA to the Book Trade by Macmillan of Canada (A Division of Canada Publishing Corporation), 164 Commander Boulevard, Agincourt, Ontario M1S 3C7; in ENGLAND by T.F.H. Publications, PO Box 15, Waterlooville PO7 6BQ; in AUSTRALIA AND THE SOUTH PACIFIC by T.F.H. (Australia), Pty. Ltd., Box 149, Brookvale 2100 N.S.W., Australia; in NEW ZEALAND by Brooklands Aquarium Ltd., 5 McGiven Drive, New Plymouth, RD1 New Zealand; in the PHILIPPINES by Bio-Research, 5 Lippay Street, San Lorenzo Village, Makati, Rizal; in SOUTH AFRICA by Multipet Pty. Ltd., P.O. Box 35347, Northway, 4065, South Africa. Published by T.F.H. Publications, Inc. Manufactured in the United States of America by T.F.H. Publications, Inc.

# Preface

Putting pen to paper and expressing the love I have for discus is not an easy task. The joy of keeping these wonderful fish is for me beyond the magic of mere words.

This guide is written out of my admiration for these fish and to help you and other discus fanciers who might gain insight from my 30 years of discus experience. I make only one request of you—once you own discus give them the best care you can and treat them like royalty, for they truly are the kings and queens of all the freshwater fishes.

Let me forewarn you now so there can be no recriminations later...discus keeping is a habit that can cost you lots of money, time, and has been known even to come between man and wife. I know you say "I can handle it." Okay, we shall see.

I would also like to point out that there are few hard-and-fast rules or methods in discus keeping. What works for me may or may not be the best procedure for you. This work is based on what I have found to work best for me in my hatchery over the past thirty-some years and is, as such, very subjective.

—JIM E. QUARLES

Discus that are healthy and cared for are outgoing, sociable, and curious.

# Introduction

These brilliant turquoise discus are one year old. They will continue to grow until they pair off and begin to spawn. Then they will stop growing.

Before we start with what a discus is and is not, I would like to say that discus and angelfish have been the most desired and sought after of all the fishes since they were first made available through importation to the world's hobbyists. They are the most beautiful of all the freshwater tropical fishes. This was true when they were first seen in the aquarium hobby and remains just as true today. In the past they were both considered difficult to keep alive for any real length of time and even more difficult to spawn. Over time, those problems were overcome by tropical fish keepers and the aquarium literature is peppered with the names of great fishkeepers like Dr. Herbert R. Axelrod, Dr. Eduard Schmidt-Focke, Mr. Jack Wattley, Mr. Adolfo Schwartz, and others, whose efforts made these great fish available and who taught us how to

*Symphysodon aequifasciatus.* This red turquoise discus shows a very good red eye and faint barring. The shape of the head is very nice.

keep them and breed them with the tremendous success that we now enjoy. I hope you, the reader, will find much useful and direct information about keeping and breeding discus fish in this book. You will, however, find very little discussion of basic aquarium techniques. It is assumed that people who are starting with discus will have enough knowledge about tropical fish in general to be able to advance to discus and provide for their basic needs.

# The Wild Discus

**Below:**
*Symphysodon
discus*, the
Heckel. The
fifth band of
the Heckel
discus
lightens in
color when
the fish is
relaxed.
Heckels
should only
be kept with
other Heckels.

Discus are members of the family Cichlidae that are native to the Amazon River basin of South America and are found naturally nowhere else in the world. They are almost perfectly round in shape, flattened, and average about five to six inches in

or pompadour fish (as they were called in the early days), started arriving in the United States. The price of these first imports was very high. Few fishkeepers could afford them and even fewer could hope to keep them alive with the equipment and knowledge of the day.

Before we get to the different species of the genus *Symphysodon*, you should know that the entire classification scheme of cichlids is currently undergoing major revisions and in the future it may be decided that this genus contains only one species and several subspecies

**Right:** The
Heckel
Discus is the
most difficult
of the wild
discus to
keep. It
does best at
low pH—in
the 4.0 to
5.5 range.

length at maturity.

The Heckel Discus was described in 1840 by the ichthyologist Dr. Johann Jacob Heckel and largely forgotten until the 1930's when wild discus,

rather than the two species with their subspecies that are now recognized. While the results of these scientific studies are interesting to anyone with a more than casual interest in discus, the fish themselves are totally unaware of them and shall continue to behave in exactly the same way they behave right now. So regardless of what they are called, you will find that all discus will breed and interbreed and crossbreed and produce young that can again crossbreed.

It is because all discus can be crossed that we have such a horror story with many of the captive-bred fish that are in the hobby today. You should be

**Above:** It is a real triumph of discus keeping to breed the wild Heckel. There are few aquarists who have the skill to do it.

**Left:** The blue Heckel.

Heckels show even light blue or light red horizontal stripes overlaying the golden base color along the body.

**Facing page:** This is a large male, the offspring of wild green discus, *Symphysodon aequifasciatus aequifasciatus.*

aware of the differences in the natural fish and the man-made, tank-bred variants. While it is true that there are some limited variations that occur in wild-type discus, these should not be of great concern to discus keepers. I have much more to say about these man-made varieties later, but first let's take a look at the natural discus types.

**THE GENUS SYMPHYSODON**

As of this writing there are said to be two discus species, *Symphysodon discus* with the subspecies *S. discus discus* and *Symphysodon discus willischwartzi*; and *Symphysodon aequifasciatus* which has three subspecies, *S. aequifasciatus aequifasciatus*, *S. aequifasciatus axelrodi*, and *S. aequifasciatus haraldi*. To the untrained eye, *S. aequifasciatus* can easily be discerned by the presence of nine dark vertical bands while *S. discus* shows three bands most prominently with the center, or Heckel band, being the most obvious. The dark bands on the discus are not always present in the same intensity. Sometimes they are almost absent and at other times, as when stressed, they can become very dark.

I think the best way to understand the diverse discus strains or color types is to start with the wild types and work our way through to the maze of discus types found in the hobby today.

*SYMPHYSODON DISCUS*

The Heckel discus, *S. discus* is the crème de la crème of the wild discus and the fish that

A first generation offspring of wild royal blue discus, or *Symphysodon aequifasciatus haraldi*.

started the discus fever worldwide. It is the original discus species described by Dr. Heckel way back in 1840. The fish was originally found at Morere in the Rio Negro. It was thought that this fish was only to be found in the Rio Negro, but has been found, albeit rarely, in the Rio Trombetas and Rio Abacaxis.

The Heckel discus comes in two color types: the red-striped Heckel and the blue-striped Heckel. They both sport the Heckel band, an accentuated middle bar and the trademark of

this discus. The bars on the Heckel can, with good care and feeding, fade and almost disappear.

Of all the wild discus, the Heckel discus is the most challenging to keep and breed. It offers the most chances for developing new strains than any of the others, but the price is high in effort and failures. The Heckel is a shy fish and should never be kept with other species of discus. It is absolutely necessary that this fish be given special water and tank conditions. It requires very soft water and must be kept at a much higher temperature than the other types of discus. The pH must also be exactly to its liking. I keep all Heckels at 5.2 to 5.6 pH and a water temperature of 92°F. I use 90% reverse osmosis water and 5% plain tap water.

This is the specimen (holotype) used to describe *Symphysodon aequifasciatus haraldi*.

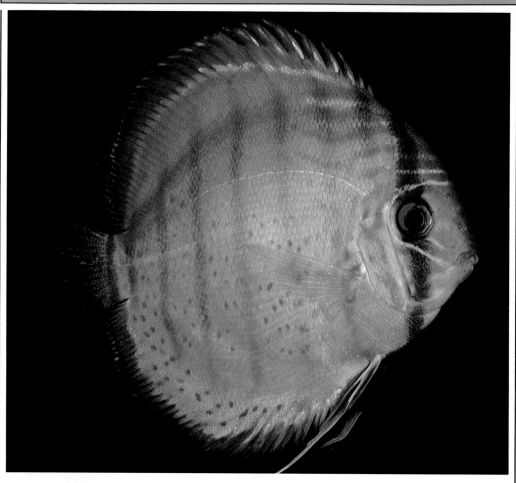

The Peruvian green discus, *Symphysodon aequifasciatus aequifasciatus.*

The remaining 5% tap water is filtered over peat.

*S. discus discus* cabeça azul (blue head) variety from the Rio Jau is a most desired fish because of its blue head and intense red coloration.

*S. discus willischwartzi,* is a rare gem in the discus hobby. It was found originally in Rio Abacaxis. Very little has been documented on this fish due to its rarity. The outstanding features of this fish are the bright blue head area and bright red stripes that run along the body. It is a beautiful fish (in the photos). I must confess that I have never seen one. I have tried for years to obtain a couple, or even one, for my hatchery, but no luck. I will keep trying as I feel that this fish offers the best hope for expanding the color types.

**SYMPHYSODON AEQUIFASCIATUS**

The wild brown discus, *S. aequifasciatus axelrodi,* is found most often near

Belem and Rio Urubu to Manaus. Over the years it has been the most commonly found discus in the hobby. The body color of the fish is yellowish brown or olive colored to rusty red. There are no lengthwise streaks on body or fins, although a few blue streaks may occur on the forehead. The eyes are red and sometimes black. The anal fin shows both red and blue streaks. The long ventral fins are brightly colored with orangeish to red and blue stripes. You will notice that there are nine black vertical bars that vary in intensity according to the mood and health of the fish.

The brown discus is easy to spawn and adjusts well to tank conditions. The spawns are quite large in most cases when the fish are in top condition and have been fed lots of live foods. Two or three hundred eggs in a spawn is not uncommon. For those who would like a natural display tank of wild discus, you could not hope for a better discus than a wild brown. They are strong fish and do very well in the home aquarium with clean water. They will adjust to tap water conditions without the need to adjust pH or hardness for breeding.

The red Alenquer discus

*S. discus willischwartzi.* This is one of the rare finds in the discus world. Many people wonder if it is a naturally occurring hybrid.

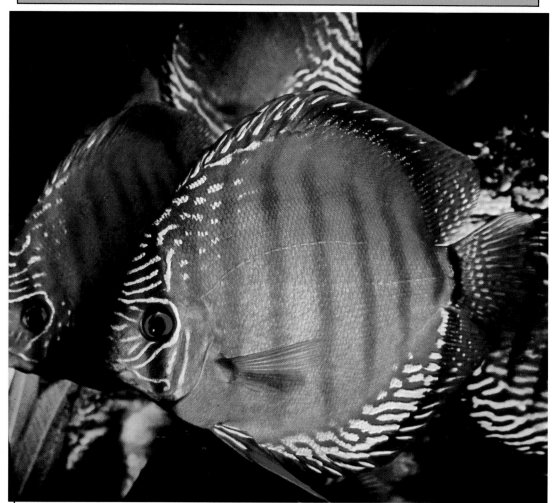

The brown discus, *Symphysodon aequi- fasciatus axelrodi*. The brown coloration can vary in intensity from a golden yellow to deep reddish brown.

is a variety of the brown discus that is very interesting as a cross-breeder. It carries a lot of rusty brown with a reddish tint and may be the key to the development of the solid red discus at some point in the future. The fins are very colorful with deep red on the anal fins and all the fins are trimmed in black.

I have found the red Alenquer easy to condition and spawn and it produces large numbers of fry. The adults are outstanding parents and will attack the net or your fingers when protecting their young. Crossing the red Alenquer with a German turquoise should produce some very interesting fry.

The blue discus, *S. aequifasciatus haraldi*, is found at Leticia, Peru, in the Purus River and near Manacapuru in Brazil. *S. aequifasciatus haraldi* appears to have two (or more) color types depending on collecting location. The blue discus shows lengthwise streaks, bright blue on a light brown background. The eye is bright red. The royal blue discus is simply a more colorful fish with more intensely colored blue stripes all over the body. These fish show nine vertical black bars with the seventh black bar through the eye area being very apparent. The dorsal and anal fins are trimmed in black.

The brown discus is the easiest of all the wild discus to acclimate to captivity. It is also the easiest of the wild discus to convince to spawn in the aquarium.

Given clean, warm water there should be no trouble in keeping the blue discus and it rates second in ease of keeping and breeding after the brown discus.

The green discus, S. *aequifasciatus aequifasciatus*, (Pellegrin discus) is found in Lake Tefé, Rio Tefé, Santarem, and the Peruvian Amazon. As with most wild stock, the brownish-yellow body is common, but the green discus is identified by lengthwise streaks, dark brown on a dark green background. The eye is reddish brown.

The Tefé variety has many red spots on its sides and is called red-spotted green in the hobby. The Tefé fish are very desirable and difficult to obtain. The royal green discus has no red but intense green stripes from head to tail. The anal fin is a bright green with red stripes throughout. The ventral fins are bright orange to red with bright green showing.

I have had a lot of green discus in my tanks over the years and the one thing I have always noticed is the bright colors, but the green discus does not always have the best body shape. I feel that with proper breeding this problem can be overcome and the

The red Alenquer is a type of brown discus. It is coveted for its intense reddish brown coloration.

breeder can produce a perfectly rounded brightly colored solid green discus. There is some exciting work going on with the green discus both in the United States and the Far East, and it is hoped that soon there will be a very bright solid green discus with a good round body and high fins to introduce to the hobby. Crossing a green discus with a German turquoise could prove to be an interesting project.

There are other color varieties that occur naturally in the wild, but so far they are all classified under the species listed above.

If you are going to keep wild-type discus, you most likely will never end up with just one type. Once you get hooked on wild fish, you will want to keep and breed them all. The possible crossings of pure

The wild royal blue discus is a *haraldi* with more diffused blue coloration. Approximately 6% of the offspring of normally colored *haraldis* are royal blues.

Green discus are hard not to like with their golden ground color and red spots.

strain wild stock and the recrossing of both wild fish and hybrids is endless but should always be done with an improvement plan in mind. If crossing is done, the work must be selective and those fry that are poor specimens must be culled and not allowed to reach the marketplace.

**WILD DISCUS IN CAPTIVITY**

If you are willing to make the commitment necessary to fulfill the needs of these wild fish, you will benefit from some understanding of what your fish goes through before it arrives in your home. Knowing something of the rigors these sensitive fish

undergo during their capture and travels will give you some clue as to their physical and emotional state when they are safely (hopefully) installed in your aquarium. Armed with this insight, you will be more likely to prepare yourself in advance for whatever special care they may

A royal blue from the Rio Purus River in Brazil.

require. Hopefully you will take to heart the published advice about their physical requirements and not attempt to keep them in conditions not consistent with their well-being.

I wish I could tell you that wild discus travel in

Another form of the royal blue discus. Even among the wild fish, there are individual differences.

streams and tributaries of the mighty queen herself, the Amazon River. Amazonian indian fishermen, the most amazing and probably the bravest in the world, must penetrate the tangled root fortresses of the discus to seize their prizes. The discus are well protected in their serene, sun-dappled habitats by the jungle banks. They are fast and elusive. Their hunters have learned that the easiest way to capture them is to strike while they are in a deep sleep. The majority of the wild discus are caught in

style on their journey out of the jungle. Like so many other dispossessed royalty, they make a very humble journey into exile from their domains in the little

the dead of night with the aid of battery-powered lamps. Even so, catching wild discus is hard labor. Discus do not school in the wild, each individual is a

This is a young brown discus, not older than six months. As he grows, the color will intensify and the shape will fill out.

prize in itself.

After capture, the wild discus are held in primitive containers by the fishermen until the riverboat arrives which will transport the fish from point to point until it reaches a fish export center like Manaus on the Rio Negro. When speaking in terms of stress and discus a long time could be a matter of hours, but these wild discus have to survive several weeks of stop-and-go travel before they arrive in the wholesalers' tanks. Needless to say, the losses are great.

When they do reach the shipping point, they are not fed and for the most part are just sorted as to size and color before being transshipped to the U.S. and other areas of the world. Given this treatment, it is little wonder that most are in a stressed and weakened condition by the time they reach the importers tanks.

The importers/wholesalers spend little time conditioning and feeding before the fish are shipped out. For the most part, the wholesalers are careful of the stock—these *are* valuable fish—but it is necessary for them to move all the fish through their establishments as quickly as possible.

With this is mind, it only stands to reason that any wild discus will require a lot of T.L.C. before any consideration can be given to their breeding. They will need above all to to have every possible stressor eliminated. They will probably need medical treatment. All wild fish have parasites. They will have to be treated before you can bring them to normal health. Specific treatments for parasites will be discussed in the following chapters. Above all, they will need rest, peace, quiet and good food. Then, we can think about breeding, or rather, they will think about breeding.

Remember also, that these are wild fish. They are not tame. They will be very surprised to find themselves in the confines of a tank. They will not like it.

Your efforts will be generously compensated. Those who devote themselves to developing the skills to properly care for wild discus will experience tremendous pleasure as they enjoy the matchless beauty of their well-conditioned fish. A master breeder will be amply rewarded as his wild discus lay their eggs and tend their precious fry. Add to all this the knowledge that you have mastered the most difficult skill of discus culture—the spawning of wild discus—and your satisfaction will be boundless.

Tefé green. All wild fish benefit from some cover in the tank at first. Bare breeding tanks can be used after the fish have settled down and chosen their mates.

# Cultivated Varieties

Pigeon bloods, the newest discus flavor for the nineties. These delightful fish are very gregarious and outgoing.

Anyone who wants to carry out a program of cross-breeding discus must remember that it takes a tremendous amount of time, space, and water. The young resulting from this type of a breeding program must be kept in large numbers for up to and beyond a year. Keeping several thousand discus for up to five months and then selecting down to 500 or more and holding these for another year requires a lot of tank space and work. If this is your cup of tea, I wish you good luck, and may you be the winner of the next discus lotto!

It is too bad that we have lost the history of all the hybrids we see in today's discus selections. Without going into great detail at this point, the reader should be on notice that most of the tank-raised discus types you will find for sale today are the results of hundreds of cross-breedings. These in turn have been crossed and recrossed. The point is that no one really knows the genetics of any of the so-called "strains." It is my feeling that there is no fixed strain of pure discus other

One of the problems with the cultivated varieties of discus is the names that are used. This is a red turquoise discus but you may find it sold under any number of more flowery names.

than the pure wild stock. Others will strongly disagree on this point. Countless breeders have developed almost cookie-cutter color types, but I will maintain until proven wrong, that even they do not know the true genetic makeup of their best strains. There are some

keepers. Certainly in the beginning, and even now for most hobbyists, anyone lucky enough to find a male and a female that would spawn and raise the fry was more than satisfied with the results. So who cared about the bloodlines of the parents? The fact that you had a spawning

very colorful and well-shaped fish out there and to some it will make little difference exactly how they got that way.

## THE DISCUS GENETICS MESS

Discus hobbyists have been breeding the king for a long time now, and the detail required to produce offspring has proven maddening to many discus

pair and they produced viable offspring was enough to make you a "discus breeder." This resulted in a very mixed gene pool among the tank-raised discus right from the beginning. Then along comes a fish that looks a little different from the mother or father, maybe one red eye and one green, and all of a sudden its a

new "strain" with a name like "turquoise double-vision pearl black super Chinese blue," and the hobbyist figures that with a name like that, they'll sell like hot cakes, right!? For a while they did, just long enough for the fouled-up gene pool to spread far and wide. Presently, we have well over one hundred "strains" of discus advertised to hobbyists. Just what constitutes the genetic makeup of any of these fish is the big question. Don't ask me, I

One of the problems with selecting discus is that we buy our fish when they are young and not fully colored.

This fish and others like it are known as red royal blue. The amount and intensity of the red coloration varies from fish to fish and other factors, such as lighting and food play an important role in how the eye perceives the color of the fish.

can assure you I do not know. Don't ask the breeder of these wonderful new "strains" unless you also believe in the tooth fairy, because they usually don't know themselves. They know what the fish they started with looked like, but the true genetics from wild stock? Forget it.

Now, all I've said about the pedigrees of the discus strains available today should not keep you from finding a strain of discus you like and starting to work with these wonderful fish. The main point I am trying to make is that if you are going to be serious and scientific about breeding discus you must start with a known wild species, a pure discus. If you have found a strain you like among the types offered, by all means go ahead and work with them, but be

aware that it's the luck of the draw as to what kind of a fish you will ultimately be keeping in your tanks. In all fairness to the breeders of domestic discus strains, I must state that a conscientious breeder could breed most of the popular strains and with proper methods develop other colors or enhancements and then fix these changes into a new line of fish.

I will be satisfied if I can convince just one person reading this to develop a real scientific interest in breeding colorful discus from wild stock with known genetic principles. For those of you who cannot start with wild fish, the best you can hope to do is find a fish you like and go on with limited knowledge available about what lines of breeding were used to improve it. (I prefer to use "color type" to describe these fish rather than the more specific term "strain.")

# The Right Discus for You

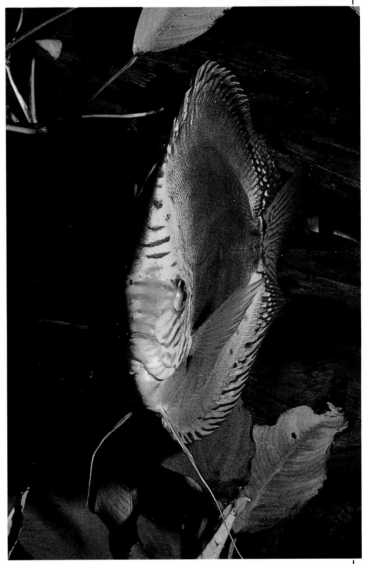

A magnificent deep blue cobalt discus.

How do you pick the right discus for you? For a newcomer to discus-keeping, the tank-raised discus you can buy from any number of reputable breeders is far and away the best fish to start out with. There are many reasons for this, but foremost is that you will find them easy to feed and grow to proper size for spawning. They were bred in captivity and have not experienced the shock of capture. The wild fish may never have seen a man before it was netted from its home. The tank-bred fish has come to trust humans. We are the source of all manner of good things, like the baby brine shrimp that were among their first foods. Tank-bred discus have not had to reconcile themselves to life within glass walls; they were born within them. They were raised in water that was modified for their health and well-being, but they have not tasted the water of the Amazon that can never be exactly

Shape is certainly an important feature in the selection of your discus. The overall impression should be that of a round fish.

duplicated for our wild fish.

Wild fish take a long time to condition to new tanks. They do not acclimate easily. The preparation of the water for wild stock is a demanding and painstaking business. Feeding wild stock is a challenge. Understandably, they don't recognize the foods we offer our aquarium fish and must be carefully weaned onto their new diet. All in all, wild fish demand lots of skill and generous amounts of time from their keepers.

## SELECTION OF YOUR STOCK

In general there are two types of discus hobbyist. One type is the person who has kept tropical fish for some time and who understands some of the basic fishkeeping rules and methods. This person has some knowledge of the water tests and treatments used to prepare water for different species of fish. Some people of this first type see discus on display and buy them on impulse. There have been no preparations made. The

Once in a rare while, you will find a fish in a spawn that has an unusual pattern. The vertical striping on the front of this turquoise is a feature that the breeder will strive to set into a true-breeding strain.

tanks are not readied, but they take the chance hoping that they can make up for that by a few changes in their present setups. They find it difficult to keep the fish alive for very long. They give up in despair and are usually the ones who spread the word that discus are hard to keep. This type of hobbyist may even try a few more times to keep discus, but in the end most of these people just give up and blame the fish.

The type-two hobbyist started to prepare himself for his discus before he even began to look for his stock. He has read every book and article available to him on the care and culture of the discus. He is learning everything he can about water chemistry, foods for discus, and discus health. He will keep and breed discus. This hobbyist has just opened the door to a joyful new world.

When you are ready to choose your discus there are basically four avenues open to you. I recommend only one.

## ADOLESCENT DISCUS

I think the best course is to buy adolescent discus in the 2.5- to 3.5-inch size range. There are a number of good reasons for this:

They are not as sensitive to changes in their environment as baby fish and will settle down much sooner. It is sometimes true that getting them to feed can be a problem, but if you add a few guppies to their tank they soon adapt and start eating again. Guppies are vigorous feeders and the discus soon catch on to the game. Once they have started to feed, you simply remove the guppies and the discus will continue to accept new foods with hearty appetite.

By the time they have reached 3.5 inches, young discus should begin to show some hint of their adult coloration. Even at this size, they will only give a good hint of their future colors. Full colors do not usually "fix" until the fish are about one year old.

Do not believe anyone who tells you they can tell the sex of discus 100% of the time. Sexing is tough and no one can be certain of the gender of a fish that has not spawned. The only true proof of the sex of a discus is the appearance of the genital papilla at spawning. There is, however, a tried and true method for increasing your chances in the discus gender roulette. From a tankful of young fish of the same spawn, choose the two largest, two middle-sized, and two smallest fish of your liking and you will probably have at least one pair. Having thus stacked the odds in your

## BABY DISCUS

Starting with very young discus has its advantages, but I do not recommend small discus (baby fish) to anyone who is new to

Lighting plays a big role in the way you see your discus' colors. It is a fallacy that discus need a dark tank. Normal tank lights do not bother discus.

favor, you will find that when they are about one year of age they will pair off and if you are very, very lucky, you will have raised three pairs. If you are very lucky, you will have two pairs, and if you are lucky, you will have one pair. Even though it will require a year's worth of care before these adolescent fish are ready to breed, this is the course I recommend as most likely to give you the best results for money spent.

discus keeping. While it is true the price is lower for very small fish, your losses will probably wipe out any savings.

## ADULT DISCUS

Another route is to buy fully developed adult discus. This, of course, is a most expensive way to start out. Adult discus have a tendency to be set in their ways and do not appreciate a move, even into a new tank. They will probably go off their food. They will

Healthy discus tame quickly and know their keeper well. They will not shy away from your hand. In fact, many discus will affectionately rub against your hand.

turn their noses up at every food you offer them for what seems to be an impossible length of time, leaving you to siphon the bottom of the tank feeding after feeding. Your water conditions will not please them and they will behave as though they are on death's door (and they may well be). They are difficult to acclimate. Suffice it to day that adult discus are just plain difficult!

Beware when offered so-called spawning pairs. These fish may be old and spawned out. The male may be infertile. They may

are tremendously valuable to their owners. Most people who have spawning pairs would not part with them for love nor money.

**WILD DISCUS**

The last method you could use to pick your breeding stock is to buy wild-caught discus. This method offers rewards to those few who will use a scientific program of breeding. However, if you are looking for a quick sale for most of the offspring from your breeding operation this is not the way to start out. Overall

eat the eggs, or they may not even be a pair at all. The more outstanding the pair, the more skeptical I would be. "Married" discus

the expense of buying wild stock is far less than any other type of discus. You can buy fully grown breeder-size wild discus for

One benefit of hand feeding is that you can make sure all the fish are getting to the food. Sometimes there is a smaller fish that can't compete and needs special rations.

Full-color turquoise are becoming very popular. There is even a strain that has no patterning anywhere on the body, not even on the face. Needless to say, this fish is very expensive.

much much less than the fancy new color types of any size. However, at the present time the market is limited for wild fish. Over the years I have culled many more fish than I have sold, and I have given away more wild stock than I've ever sold. It is to be hoped that someday soon the demand for high grade wild fish will develop again.

**WHAT TO LOOK FOR**

Discus are pretty clear

about it when they are not feeling well. A sick discus looks sick and a healthy discus looks great! When selecting your discus, avoid fish that are dark in color. Darkening of the body is one of the clearest signs that all is not right with a discus. Watch out for skittish fish as well. If the fish hide when the tank is approached, this is a sign that the water quality is bad or the fish are sick. Apathy, as well, is a bad sign. If the fish doesn't react to your presence, chances are it is pretty sick, even if it looks all right otherwise.

Adolescent discus should be showing signs of their adult shape. They will still have slightly pointed noses, but their bodies should be beginning to fill out. They should look well fed. Their bellies should look full, but not protruding. Look for "razorbacks." Fish with a thin dorsal area and huge eyes for their body size are damaged and will always be stunted.

Their eyes should be bright and alert looking regardless of color. Most people go for the fish with the bright red eyes, but amber eyes are also acceptable. As long as the eyes are clear and bright, not clouded or protruding, the color is not a decisive factor. Clouding of the eye is often the result of abrasions suffered during transport, but can indicate a more serious bacterial or

Amber eyes can be just as attractive as red eyes, especially if the amber compliments the color of the fish.

fungal infection as well, so it is best to avoid fish with eyes that are not clear.

The skin and fins should be totally intact. There should be no cuts or abrasions, reddened areas, white patches, white spots, or sloughing of the skin slime. Unless you know your fish pretty well and can be certain that a skin

Look for a beautiful rounded profile. Highly iridescent turquoise discus are gorgeous as the colors change in the light.

defect is minor and easily treated, avoid the fish with less than perfect skin.

Both gills should be working as a team, about one gill-beat per second. Rapid breathing is normal if the fish is excited by food or the chase, but a calm fish should not be hyperventilating. One-sided breathing is not good and could indicate an infestation with gill flukes. Watch out also for gill deformities. Fish with

missing or curled gill covers are culls and will pass on these defects to their offspring.

**THE PRICE YOU PAY**

One point to remember about good discus stock—it is not cheap no matter what size you choose. Expect to pay a reasonable price for your initial stock. There is no advantage to buying junk fish. There are hundreds of sincere discus breeders from whom you can select your youngsters. Most are honest and dedicated hobbyists who put great skill into developing the best fish that they can. Some, however, are not so honest and some are outright crooks. Deal only with known honest dependable breeders. This is the only way you can be sure of getting a good start with discus.

**ONE SIMPLE RULE**

Never keep a lone discus in a tank. Discus are not schooling fish in the wild, but they are found most often as pairs or pairs with fry. In the unnatural surroundings of the aquarium, however, a single fish will weaken and die. Discus are shy fish that prefer to hide in darkened areas in nature. They should be offered private areas in the home aquarium as well. It is important that your discus have no fear of you or their environment. For best results they should be hand-tame and willing to eat from your fingers. I try to tame my discus to the point where they will lay in my hand when I place it in

Red turquoise is one of the most popular discus colors. This variety is usually available at a reasonable price.

always best to place two or more discus together.

**ANOTHER GOOD RULE**
You must earn the trust of your discus. It is most the tank. This takes time and patience, but the rewards are well worth the effort both for you and lots of happy spawns later on.

# The Physical Requirements

### GENERAL HEALTH CONSIDERATIONS

It is no secret that discus are special fish or that they have special needs. As a discus keeper you must be aware of the nature and specific requirements of

Pet shops carry a wide range of water conditioners to remove chlorine and chloramines. Photo courtesy of Hagen.

this fish. If you ever hope to enjoy success with discus, you must be able to evaluate the condition of your fish on a regular basis.

When discus are not feeling well or their tank or water conditions are out of order, they will show signs that indicate the need for rapid and effective action on the part of the hobbyist.

The first warning beacon to the hobbyist is a general darkening of the fish. This is a clear sign that all is not well with the fish. Even though discus are extremely variable in their color intensity, a darkened fish is a fish in trouble. If something is badly wrong, this can happen within minutes. When discus are well, they are robust, hardy fish. When they are not well, they deteriorate so quickly that the hobbyist must always be on the lookout for any abnormal darkening of any discus.

### CLEAN WATER

Clean water, more than any other element in the care of your fish, will help you preserve the health of your fish. There will still be occasional problems even when your fish are kept under the best of conditions, but since prevention is the key, clean water essential. If your fish are showing signs of trouble, fast treatment is mandatory. Look first to your water and if that checks out okay, start

You can purchase cultures to seed your biological filter. Photo courtesy of Hagen.

digging for other clues immediately.

There are many people who say you should change this percentage or that percentage of water every day, week, or month. If this is what they do, that's fine. You must change your water *before* it becomes dirty. The amount and frequency of your water changes depend mostly on how many fish are in how many gallons of water and how much and what kinds of food you are giving them. One thing is certain, however, you must change your water.

## WATER CHEMISTRY

The chemistry of discus water will make all the difference whether or not you are able to spawn your discus once they are matched or paired. It is also a factor long before your fish reach breeding age. Discus kept in very hard water while they grow from fry to adults may never be able to reproduce. Hard water reduces the males' ability to produce sperm. Young fish that are to be used for breeding should be kept in moderate to soft water until they pair off. Discus in the wild are found in very very soft, acidic water. The softness of the water is the result of heavy rainfall and the effect of peat-like substances over which the water flows. A natural pH of 4.8 to 5.8 is common in the areas where they are found.

In my hatchery I make great efforts to keep all my discus in very soft water. Those that are to be sold and shipped are conditioned to water of 10 German degrees of hardness before sale. Otherwise, they remain in water with a hardness of 5 to 6 degrees German hardness. Conditioning water to this softness requires a water treatment program of some type in most cases.

I use a fairly large reverse osmosis system combined with large peat filters.

## IDEAL WATER CONDITIONS

The ideal water would have a hardness of 1°DH.

The pH would be 5.8, and there would be 100 percent filtration at all times. You will never reach the perfect water condition in any aquarium, but you should try to keep it as close to the ideal as possible at all times. One way to approach the ideal is to perform frequent water changes.

## WATER CHANGES

I recommend that you replace 25 to 50 percent of your water in rearing tanks

If you are going to keep plants with discus, you must be very careful not to overfertilize the plants.

every day. In spawning tanks, replace 50 percent of the water each week. These recommend changes do not have to be done all at one time. Partial water changes over time are better than full changes all at once. I change a little water in the morning and more at night.

## PEAT

Peat is tremendously helpful in the conditioning of your water for discus. Use peat to treat and soften the water. Peat gently acidifies your water with natural humic acids similar to those that keep the home waters of discus so acidic. Pure peat untainted with pesticides is simple magic in the spawning of discus. Filtering your aquarium water through peat will adjust and control the pH of your water, and as an added bonus will remove some of the harmful elements in the water. Peat filtration will turn your water a slight tea color but that is a small price to pay for both pH and disease control. Take care, however, to check your pH often when using peat. It is a very efficient substance for acidifying water and you should be careful not to overdo it. If you notice that your pH is dropping, ask yourself if you have been feeding heavily and perhaps missed a couple of water changes. Peat

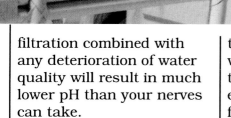

filtration combined with any deterioration of water quality will result in much lower pH than your nerves can take.

### REVERSE OSMOSIS

Reverse osmosis is remarkable in its ability to remove the elements that make your water hard. It also removes chlorine and does a fine job on removing other toxins from the water as well. The only problem with reverse osmosis water is that it is too clean—empty of trace elements. You must add back some trace elements to your R.O. water before use. Thirty percent dechlorinated tap water mixed with the R.O. water will do nicely. Follow

the remixing of the water with peat filtration (Check the pH!) and you will have excellent water conditions for your discus.

### EQUIPMENT

The nuts and bolts of discus keeping are found in the equipment necessary to keep and breed the fish. To some extent, the equipment choices will depend upon the extent of your breeding program. Hobbyists keeping only a few fish simply for the pleasure of watching and learning about discus will not need the same kind of equipment as the person who envisions a well-planned breeding and production project. No one

There are so many designer tanks on the market these days that you can go all out and design a real fantasy tank as long as the needs of the fish come first.

type of equipment is absolutely right or wrong; I can only outline general principles and make general recommendations.

### TANKS

For keeping discus in the show or community tank, you should allow at least 15 gallons per adult fish. It is possible to keep discus in relatively good health in a community set-up if you are very careful in your choice of tankmates and do not expect more than to keep your discus. Breeding in a furnished tank is strictly a hit-or-miss affair, and to risk the cliché, you can't have your cake and eat it. If you want simply to observe the beautiful discus in a fully furnished tank, by all means do so, but if you expect to be able to keep and rear the young, you must be willing to forego the decorations, driftwood, and gravel.

Breeder tanks should be no smaller than 20 gallons. The best I've found are custom-made 60-gallon tanks that measure 24"x 24"x24". I have used standard 30-gallon tanks, but the larger size permits excellent control of water conditions and lighter cleaning work on a day-to-day basis. Whatever size breeder tank you select, remember that the otherwise adequate 20-gallon rectangle may not physically accommodate your adult discus. Among the larger discus, an adult male of 8 inches is not too uncommon. They need the extra room to turn and swim. I have seen breeders perform in standard 20-gallon show tanks but would not crowd my fish in this manner.

In addition to the breeder tanks you will need grow-out tanks for the fry when they are ready to be moved from the company of their parents. I do use 20-gallon tanks for this until the fry are the size of a quarter. When they reach this size, I leave the smaller of the lot in the 20-gallon tank for extra feeding and move the larger fry to 100 gallon tanks. My custom-made tanks are 48"x 24"x24" for growing out these fry. With the amount of breeding I do, I have eight of these larger tanks and sort the fry every three weeks to keep only fish of the same size together. This is to make sure that the smaller weaker fish are not picked on and when I see fry that are undersized I make extra effort to feed these fish more often and a higher grade of food. In most cases, this will allow them to develop just as

well as their faster-growing brothers and sisters.

I use only bare-bottom tanks for breeding or rearing fry. There is no gravel or ornamentation whatsoever. I use a sponge filter or several depending on the volume of water and the fish load. I keep the air volume low in the breeder tanks and high in the rearing tanks. On the 100-gallon rearing tanks I also have two power filters mounted on the sides of the tanks as well. You will find that keeping the water super clean in your grow-out tanks will have your

**Far left:** Water changes are essential to the health of your discus. Photo courtesy of Aquarium Products.

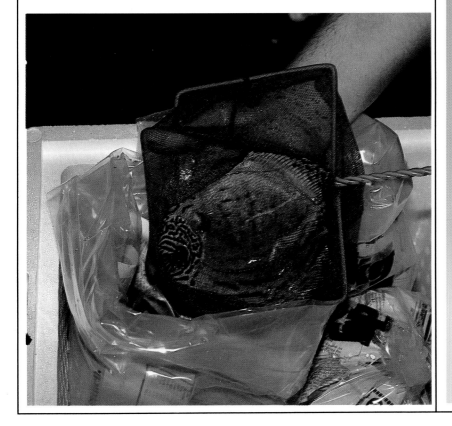

**Left:** Nets are more important than you think. The larger the net, the easier it is to catch the fish. Also, it is easy to damage a fish with a small net. Be sure to sterilize nets before using them on another tank.

Submersible heaters placed near the bottom of the tank ensure that you won't accidentally break the heater during your water changes. Photo courtesy of Hagen.

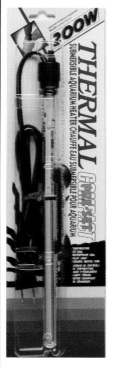

young discus showing phenomenal growth and excellent health.

## HEATERS

Your discus must be kept in water that is over 84°F and under 90°F at all times. I run my breeders at 84 constant degrees. The rearing tanks are kept at 86°F.

You should buy only the very best aquarium heater you can get, period. I really believe that submersible heaters are the best. I buy the best and have never had a run-away heater in any of my tanks since I started spending the little extra to buy top-of-the-line heaters. (Warning: It *can* happen.) And, as simple as it may be, a good aquarium thermometer is a real life-saver.

## FILTERS
### Undergravel Filters

Undergravel filters are common and most of you have used these before at some time of another. Some of you, I am sure, are still using them. I feel that unless you are setting up a large display tank, you should not use undergravel filters with discus and never in a spawning tank. There is plenty of information in the literature about undergravel filters, so I won't go into the details here. I will, however, make one very flat statement. . . those who use undergravel filters will suffer more dead and diseased discus than those people who avoid them.

### Sponge Filters

I prefer the simple foam sponge filter above all other methods of filtration. I mount the filter off the floor of the tank so that it will not trap any uneaten food beneath it and the tank can be kept very clean with little effort.

If you are using an outside power filter or a canister filter, a sponge prefilter will be a tremendous asset. The prefilter will trap the waste matter and prevent it from clogging the filter media in the power or canister filter, enabling them to remain undisturbed for long periods of time and enabling them to very

Internal power filters can be used on a discus tank. Photo courtesy of Danner.

efficiently remove nitrogenous compounds from the water.

When washing the sponge filters do not use tap water. Use aged water to avoid killing off the bacteria that form the basis of your biological action. Do not use hot water; use only lukewarm water. Just squeeze out the filter a few times and be sure to return it to the same tank.

### Wet-Dry Filter

After the sponge filter, the next best filter arrangement has to be the wet-dry drip type. With this type of filter, you arrange for the water to splash through high-surface-area filtering media and drip or be pumped back into the tank. Before allowing the water to reach the filter media, you can use a foam rubber sponge pad    as a prefilter to collect the solids from the water and then clean this pad as needed. If properly arranged, this type of filter can run for very long periods of time without needing to be broken down for cleaning.

### Box Filter

The inside or outside box (power) filter is another tool that can be used to clean discus water. I find them useful for the removal of solids from the water, but not of much use for biological filtration because they need cleaning too often to allow real lasting biological action. (Unless

German "Wattley" female.

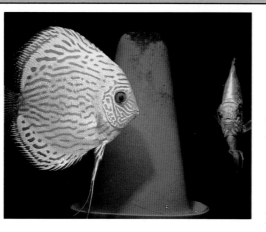

they are equipped with a sponge prefilter, which will extend their time span between cleanings.)

**Drip System**
The constant drip system involves the constant replacement of tank water with fresh water or a filtered water drip line from a supply outside the system. To make this system work you will need to tap your tanks at the waterline with a discharge tube that drains away the outflow of water or transfers it to an outside filter system. Valves on each tank supply new water at a constant rate. The volume of this water can be different in any or all tanks depending on just how much flow or exchange of water you desire. I have used such a custom-made arrangement and find it very useful when conditioning wild discus to their new home. With this system I add a peat filter in the line and the pH problem is 100 percent solved and safe.

There are plenty of other methods and devices that can be used in filtration and lots of homemade improvements that can be added to all the above. Experiment for yourself and I am sure you can design your own.

There are products at your pet shop that will safely lower the pH of your water. Photo courtesy of Fritz.

# Maintenance

## TESTING THE WATER

Your water test kit is your friend. Use it often. It will confirm that you are keeping up with a proper schedule of water changes and it will tell you if you are not. The tests for nitrite and nitrates are very important until you get a

pH and hardness are also crucial. You cannot keep discus properly without them.

## FILTER UPKEEP

Remember to clean your prefilters and filters often.

This is very important in fry and rearing tanks

You cannot have healthy discus like this if you do not attend to the maintenance of the tank. Follow the rules and your fish will reward you with their vigor.

handle on how often and how much water you need to change in your particular circumstances. Ammonia is not a factor at a pH of below 7, but should your pH rise for any reason, ammonium is converted to more-toxic ammonia almost immediately! The tests for

because of the build-up of food waste. Fry need to be fed often and generously. Even the most diligent siphoner will miss a lot of the leftover food, brine shrimp nauplii in particular, and the build-up of decaying brine shrimp can send your water quality into a downward spiral in a hurry.

### Cycling the Filter

New discus keepers often encounter massive water quality problems. Their enthusiasm is their undoing. In their desire to provide optimum conditions, they often end up sabotaging themselves. While it is necessary to

Outside power filters are easy to use and maintain. Photo courtesy of Danner.

provide clean water and lots of good food, perpetual "New Tank Syndrome" is a big problem for many. The scenario goes something like this: The aquarist sets up his tank by the book with no gravel, a new filter and new water. The clean water runs through the clean filter for about a week and everything looks great! The pH is lowered and the water is softened.

Everything looks great! The fish are added. Everything looks great! Since it is recommended that discus be fed beefheart and shrimp and other good foods, these are generously added. The fish eat of the food, some is siphoned off, and the rest lands in the new filter. The next day your nose tells you everything is not so great, so you change approximately 50 percent of the water and feed your fish. Within a few hours, your clean water is clouding up and your nose again tells you things are not so great. Your fish aren't too happy about the situation either! You know about cycling your tank, but in your desire to provide the best care for your discus, you have set yourself up for failure. The discus tank, like any other, must be allowed time to mature and the filter must be allowed time to colonize the nitrobacters in order to function properly. The large water changes recommended for the discus tank are only to be performed after the tank has had time to cycle

will be able to better understand why so much filtration and such large and frequent water changes are always advised for the discus aquarium.

without fish in residence. If you do not let your filter mature, you will never be able to provide good water for your discus. There are commercially prepared cultures of nitrobacters available at your pet shop. They are helpful in getting a good head of steam going on your filter bacteria.

There is one drawback to the way we keep discus in the breeding aquarium—no gravel. The gravel bed does serve a purpose in the show tank in that it—along with the filter—is home to the nitrifying bacteria that help to keep the water clear of unhealthy build-ups of ammonia and nitrite. If you consider that the gravel bed performs a function in the show tank that is lacking in the discus aquarium, you

If you are 100 percent sure your water is clean, clean it some more and then change some more water! If you would drink the water in your discus tank, it's clean enough...maybe. You can never keep the water in your discus tanks as clean as it should be, but try!

**Keeping the Filter Cycled**

Once you have that wonderfully useful colony

A school of beautifully matched turquoise discus. You may notice that one fish dominates the tank. Rather than remove the bully (who may be a super male looking for a worthy mate) move the lowest fish in the pecking order.

of nitrobacters multiplying and working inside your filter, it is natural not to want to disturb them, but you're going to have to service your filter sometime. The nitrifying bacteria are pretty hardy really, certainly hardier than the fish they are serving. You just have to take their simple needs into consideration when you do perform the maintenance necessary for the proper functioning of your filter. First, they don't like hot water, nor do they like cold water. Lukewarm tank water they like. So if you have to rinse any part of your filter, keep a bucket of tank water handy. Second, they don't like to be lonely. When you're changing your filter media, don't change it

all at the same time. If you can, just rinse it gently and reuse it. Leave some of the old media to keep the colony going. New filter material is useless for anything except mechanical filtration until it has been colonized with bacteria. Third, they like oxygen. The oxygen they need is carried by the water that flows through the filter to be cleaned. Be sure that there isn't a build-up of silt in the filter that will obstruct the free flow of water to your filter media. If your power goes out, the oxygen supply in your filter will be used up in a very short time and your bacteria are going to suffocate and die off. When the power comes back on...the aquarium is flooded with poison! Therefore, any time the filter is off, even for an hour, the filter material and canister must be thoroughly rinsed before it is permitted to come in contact with the aquarium water.

**CLEAN THE GLASS!**
It is very important that

Put the finishing touches on your tank maintenance when you clean the outside of the tank. Photo courtesy of Python.

you wipe the inside of the glass, front, back, sides, and what most people forget, the bottom—ON A DAILY BASIS—to remove the slime that collects! Discus give off a body slime that is used both to feed the fry and protect the skin. This slime collects on the glass, filter tubing, and filter. This slime, unfortunately, is a   perfect breeding ground for bacteria. In fry tanks, even a slight buildup of this coating can cause losses on a massive scale. Try to just develop the habit of wiping down the inside glass surfaces after each feeding as you clear the food off the bottom. I use foam rubber pads for this and find they work quite well. Never use a pad in different tanks unless you sterilize the pad before reuse. The same rule applies for nets, hoses, or any kind of equipment that would be moved from tank to tank. Don't forget the most basic rule: Wash your hands and arms when placing them in the water or going from tank to tank for any reason.

You should have and use water test kits. Photo courtesy of Fritz.

# The Proper Feeding of Discus

Your discus will eat out of your hand without hesitation when they begin to recognize you.

An excellent indication of the health of your discus is its appetite. Adult discus should be constantly looking for food. Baby discus should have bulging stomachs at all times. Any behavior. Often when discus are first brought home, they will fast for a time. Most fish won't eat when they are stressed and discus are no exception. They do get set in their ways and dislike change. Small portions of frozen blood-worms should bring them around in no time. Just be very careful to remove any uneaten

food within an hour. You don't want water quality problems, especially with new fish that are just getting used to their new homes. As I mentioned before, a few guppies in the tank will also stimulate the fish to eat. They *are*

shortage of food in the early days, and you will have stunted discus for life.

### FEAST OR FAST?
One of the first signs of trouble with discus is when it goes off its food; this is inconsistent with discus

Turkey heart, calf heart, or beef heart are excellent growth foods for discus. There are several commercial blends on the market these days, all excellent.

competitive when it comes to food.

There are many foods that your discus will eat with relish once they have been given a chance to get a taste for them. If a discus doesn't recognize a new food, it will probably turn its nose up at the unfamiliar fare. Sometimes you have to be a little bit sneaky to get your discus to accept a new menu item. It's easy. Just mix a small percentage of the new food with bloodworms or any other food they accept. Increase the percentage of the new food item until the fish are fully accepting of it.

Variety is important in the discus diet just as it is for us humans. Few wild fish eat the same thing meal after meal. Such specialized feeding reduces their chances for survival. What would happen if suddenly the special food were to disappear? Extinction! No, wild discus are not so picky. They eat anything they can get— midge larvae, small crustaceans, even fruits.

## FOODS FOR DISCUS

The most popular foods for discus are brine shrimp, heart, daphnia, mosquito larvae, bloodworms, whiteworms, glassworms, and chopped earthworms.

### Tubifex or Not?

Some people feed live tubifex and blackworms. I do not. If you feed them even one time your fish will develop tapeworms and

Baby discus are *always* hungry. Food tablets will keep them occupied for a good while. The tablets stay put when you press them against the glass, so there is less mess to clean up.

cannot be expected to live much beyond three years. You may even be able to develop good spawning pairs but all will show signs of a weakened condition. Some breeders consider this just part of the cost of having fast growth and quick spawns. I suggest that you read all you can find about tubifex worms. Talk with other discus keepers and then make up your own mind about this food source. Some use tubificids and some do not. Just ask before you buy your starters if they have ever been fed tubificids. There are treatments for tapeworms but none are 100 percent effective. Tapeworms aside, if you ever saw the fish leeches in a shipment of tubificids, you would really get an eye-opener. Not a sight for the fainthearted! There are many other reasons to avoid tubificids—heavy metals, bacteria, parasites—all of them potentially disastrous.

**Foods From the Pet Shop**

Flake, pellets, tablets, and other commercial foods are all good for discus. Many people seem to think that discus are too rare and special to eat commercially prepared foods. Some books and even discus breeders will tell you that discus will not eat flake foods. Nonsense! Discus are easy to train to eat anything and they develop a real taste for flakes. Even wild-caught discus will eat flake food if kept with other discus that eat it. There are a lot of advantages to using prepared foods as *part* of your discus' diet. If you are a working person, the convenience is very important. Prepared foods in moderation are usually relatively non-polluting, especially when compared to meaty foods like heart. It's far better to sprinkle a bit of flake in the tank in the morning than to overdo feeding a heart and shrimp mixture and have decomposing meat in the aquarium all day.

## Home Cooking

Meaty foods, properly prepared, are the true growth foods for discus. Some breeders use beefheart. Even though no wild discus ever ate beefheart in nature, this certainly is a food that discus really go wild over. Some breeders are going with calf rather than beef heart in the hope that the animal will have been exposed to fewer hormones and chemicals during its shorter life. Either way, bovine heart is rich and puts great size on discus. The other side of the coin is that it is very polluting and can foul your water in no time flat. If you are feeding beef or calf heart or a heart mixture, set up a schedule for yourself based on the regular times of your water changes. The closer you are to changing the water, the more generous you can afford to be with meaty foods. If you have just changed the water, feed lighter, cleaner foods.

My regular meat formula consists of beef heart and chicken livers mixed with peeled shrimp, oatmeal, and squash, and green baby foods and vitamins all blended together in a food processor. This mixture is

If you handfeed your fish, you will be able to gauge how much they really eat. Once you know this, you don't have to worry so much about overfeeding.

Discus like a light meal. Flake foods are part of a rounded diet for your discus. Photo courtesy of Hagen.

You can even train wild fish to handfeed with frozen bloodworms. This will certainly help them settle in and get over any initial shyness.

then placed in plastic bags, pressed into a very thin layer, and frozen. When it's time to feed, I just break off what I need and put the rest back in the freezer. Again, this food is hard on water quality, so be prepared to siphon off any leftovers you can see. If you feed sparingly and often, you should not have any problems using this wonderful, obviously delicious, food.

## VITAMINS

B-complex vitamins are the most important for discus. If the vitamin supplement you are using contains B1, B2, B5, B6, and B12, folic acid, nicotinic acid, and Vitamin E, you can be pretty secure that your fish are getting the necessary vitamins for growth, tissue repair, and reproduction.

## LIVE FOODS

Live foods are well known to be the best for getting discus into prime spawning condition, but considering the dangers associated with every type other than live brine shrimp, I prefer to condition my breeders with my beefheart and chicken liver mixture plus flake foods. Earthworms are also excellent food. Cut to size for your fish.

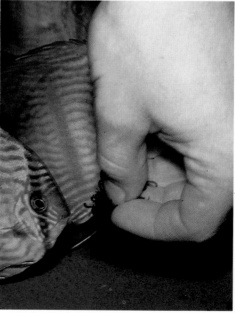

# Breeding Discus

## WHY BREED DISCUS?

It's no secret to anyone who's heard the word "discus," that these are fish that have some pretty clear likes and dislikes. It is very simple for us to understand that in the wild, discus live in highly specialized habitats, after all, they are very advanced fish, what with both mother and father feeding and caring for their young as they do. The enjoy their water, which varies only slightly from one discus locale to another, warm, soft, acidic—pure. They have lived in abundance in their native waters for centuries uncounted. They have gotten used to things being pretty much they way they always have been.

There is one sad fact, and that is that things will never again be the way they always have been on the globe we share with discus and so many other good things. When men march in the name of progress we often lose the little places where the wild things live.

It's no secret to any of us that the Amazonian rain forest (There, I've said it.) is losing ground daily. It just

*This* is why we breed discus! There are few people so jaded that they are not moved by the inexpressible beauty of the discus family behavior.

happens that the Amazonian rain forest is also the home of the wild discus. The small streams and even the great rivers are being poisoned by the advance of civilization.

It is realistic to prepare for imminent scarcity of discus and other Amazonian fishes as the

Both parents guard their eggs.

fishermen must go further and further to collect the fishes that give them their livelihood. I feel it will not be long before few, if any, wild fishes are available to export out of the country.

There are many reasons to consider spawning wild discus but perhaps the most compelling one is to keep the wild stock alive in our tanks after they become unavailable at any price and perhaps even gone forever from their native waters.

## ON GETTING PAIRS

How do you get a mated or spawning pair of discus if you can't tell the boys from the girls until they have already spawned? This is the big question. The only *sure* way to sex discus is to have a pair spawn before your eyes. Only when you see the female lay the eggs and the male fertilize them can you be 100 percent sure which is the male and which is the female. Of course, you can have your suspicions and you might be right, but you might also be wrong.

Some long-term breeders do get very good at sexing their fish. When dealing

with larger fish, it is not uncommon for the experienced breeder to be right about 80 percent of the time. No one can pick the sex of discus under young adult size and no one is right 100 percent of the time at any age. There are, however, techniques

Discus will lay eggs in a community tank, but it is rare for any fry to survive.

If you get a spawn in the rearing tank, place a divider between the parents and cone and the rest of the fish. You may be able to save the fry.

that can be used to help you pick a male and a female that are likely to develop into a good pair. Some discus experts will tell you that fish with a more pointed nose or larger lips are males or that the larger fish is a male, or that the one with the pointed fins is a male. This might work if all the fish are siblings of the same spawn, but it is still not absolute.

The best way to sex discus is to put six or eight nearly grown fish together in a 50-gallon tank with spawning cones or lengths of upright PVC pipe. (I use fire-clay bricks that are light brown to gray in color.

It is easy to see the eggs and wriggler fry on these and they are easy to keep clean.) Feed the fish properly and keep the water conditions at their best and they will tend to pair off all by themselves. They know among themselves who is male and who is female. Between discus there is always a contest going on to see who is top dog. You can use this habit to help you pick the most likely male and female. The stronger pair will pick out an area and take over. They will guard the cone or PVC in that area of the tank and chase off all the others. When you

see them starting to clean the cone or PVC pipe is time to move them into their own spawning tank. When they are settled into their new tank and have started to display cleaning behavior, do not move them again. Once a pair has been moved, it will take

The fry get more independent as they grow.

them anywhere from one week to two years for them to settle down in their tank and every time they are moved they have to start all over again. Moving a pair puts a real stress on the fish. You may even break the pair bond forever.

At times I have had to remove one parent from the tank for the sake of the fry. Some parents will fight over who will take care of the fry and the fighting can result in loss of the fry unless the best parent is selected and the weaker one removed. I have never had this result in the breaking of a pair

The parents will usually move the newly hatched wrigglers. Sometimes you will think the fry have disappeared, but the parents will simply have moved the whole spawn to a dark corner.

The parents try very hard to keep the fry on the cone, constantly picking them up in their mouths and spitting them back until they ultimately move to the parents' sides to feed.

bond. When the two are again placed together they seem not to have noticed the recent event. If you read other books on discus you can find all kind of suggestions about pair formation.

Another method for determining a pair is to place the fish you suspect as male and female into their own tank and let them settle down for a few days. Then add a third fish to the tank. If you find that one or both pick on the third fish, then you most likely have a pair. Be careful with the third fish. You should keep a close watch and if this fish is really getting a beating, take it out of the tank

The spawning act is like a slow-motion dance with the female laying the eggs and the male following to fertilize them. This is just the beginning, so don't count your eggs before they hatch!

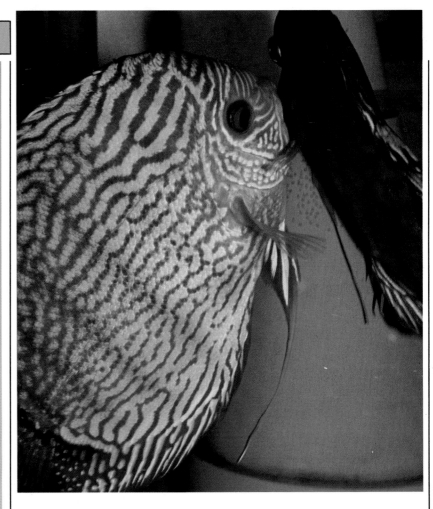

before it's damaged. The pair could even kill the third fish if it's left too long in their company. A little fin damage is to be expected, but if the skin is damaged watch for fungus until the wound is healed. Your good judgment will keep you from letting the pair damage the test fish. Getting the discus paired off is, to me, the hardest part of the whole breeding operation.

**THE SPAWNING TANK**

The spawning tank should be 30 gallons or more and over 14 inches high, but less than 26 inches high. This tank should be wide. No gravel or any other type of substrate should be used. A sponge filter of proper size should be in place and have been running long enough to be well colonized with nitrifying bacteria. A suitable spawning surface should be in place. The water should be acidic with a pH of about 5.8 to 6.3; hardness should be less than 6 ppm dGH. The softer the water, the better. Ideal conditions require peat-filtered water. Once the fish are in residence, any leftover food should be siphoned off one hour after every meal.

## COURTSHIP

When the spawning tank has been set up and is sufficiently cycled, the pair of discus are introduced and allowed to settle into their new home. With any luck and if your judgment was correct in selecting a male and female you can observe the flirting and courtship behavior of your discus. Even the most compatible pairs will exhibit behavior that seem aggressive—lip-locking, tail-slapping, and head-butting. This is usually just the prelude to romance and should not be interfered

This is a beautifully matched pair of turquoise. It's very good when the fish are close in size.

with unless things start to get really serious with one fish appearing to suffer injury. It could be that a mistake has been made and there are really two males in the tank!

The pair will spend most of their time in the immediate vicinity of the spawning place. They will both vigorously clean the cone with their mouths and this is a sure sign that spawning will begin soon. Both prospective parents take part in the cleaning activities. This can take a day or a week, but when they are ready, the female will make a few trial runs up the surface of the PVC or clay cone as if she is laying eggs. Just prior to spawning both fish will undergo a marked color change with the body darkening and the dorsal fin becoming almost black. The breeding tubes will descend just prior to spawning. The female's ovipositor is quite large and blunt. The male's breeding tube is shorter and more slender and tapers to a point.

### SPAWNING

When the time is right and the female is convinced that the spawning substrate is clean enough, she will start laying her eggs a few at a time in single rows. Usually, she will move to one side so the male can make his run over the eggs, but sometimes the pair will lay and fertilize simultaneously. Now you really know you have a pair! The number of eggs laid depends largely on the age and condition of the female, with a prime female being capable of laying as many as 200 to 300.

### Egg Eating

Unlike many other early-bird fish that spawn at dawn, discus tend to spawn towards the end of the day. This is handy if you want to watch them spawning. If you can observe quietly without upsetting the fish, do so. Be very careful with your movements. If upset, the pair will eat the eggs as fast as they are deposited. Sometimes a young pair will spawn and eat the eggs within 24 hours. This happens and there is not much you can do about it. Just wait and let them keep spawning. They should repeat the spawn about every 10 days. If the pair keeps eating the eggs, try removing the male as carefully as you can and let the female tend the eggs. If she is the egg-eater, next time remove her and let the male tend house. I have had pairs spawn up to ten times and eat every single egg. Then they stopped eating the eggs and became great parents. You can also make a wire cover to slip over the surface containing take turns fanning them with their pectoral fins and picking off any dead eggs. After about two days, the eggs hatch and are held in place by "cement glands" on their heads that secrete

the spawn so that they can still see the eggs and tend the eggs, but cannot reach the eggs to eat them. By the time the fry hatch out into "wrigglers" they have bonded to them and protect them ferociously.

**Hatching**

Once the eggs are laid, the male and female will a sticky mucus. Any fry that drop off the substrate are immediately caught in the mouths of the parents and returned to the nest. The fry will spend about the next 24 hours wriggling wildly on the spawning substrate. During their time as wrigglers they live on the food stored in their clearly visible yolk sacs.

Good parents will tend the eggs very carefully, staring and fanning while they incubate.

There are usually a few white eggs in every spawn. These are infertile and will not hatch. The rest of the spawn is doing well as the eggs become progressively darker until they hatch.

**Free-Swimming Fry**

Over the course of the next day or so, the fry become more and more independent of the spawning cone and constantly wriggle free. The parents try in vain to replace each one as it frees itself from the cone, but in the end must give up. Rather than trying to return the fry to the cone each time, the adult (usually the father)

the fry will have clustered at their mother's side and graze contentedly from her slime. As the mother's slime is depleted, the father takes over and with a neat bit of body language, signals to the fry to come to his side. The fry move *en masse* to their father and begin to nurse on his sides as well, tearing little shreds of skin and slime that contains all the nutrition they will need

catches the fry and spits it close to the body of the mother who hovers near the spawning site. Within a short period of time, all

at this stage of their lives. Because they feed continuously, the babies grow quickly and have constantly full bellies.

When the fry start to round out and become more independent of their parents, it is time to move them to their own quarters. They should be taking brine shrimp regularly before you move them.

### Use of a Night Light

The survival of the fry depends upon their feeding constantly from their parents' sides, and in the first four to five days, they must be able to easily find the nursing parent. Many young discus get lost as they try to transfer from mother to father in a dark tank. A dim light over the tank at night will help the young to find their parents. Some breeders totally cover the tank to ensure that the family isn't disturbed, but leave a small hole for a light to shine through.

### Feeding the Fry

Prepare yourself to offer newly hatched brine shrimp to the fry when they are about four to five days old. This means you should prepare your shrimp hatchers so you will have fresh shrimp ready every four hours to offer the youngsters. Harvest the shrimp and rinse them in fresh water, then squirt a small cloud of shrimp near the fry with a clean baster. The first or second time this food is offered, it will probably be ignored, but don't give up. The fry will soon recognize the brine shrimp as delicious food and feast on them until their bellies are swollen pink with brine shrimp. Be very careful about not overfeeding for the first week to ten days. You must still clean the tank bottom as before, but take great care not to suck up the young. In any case, they will hang still and close to the adults while you work in the tank. Be very careful not to overly disturb the family as you perform necessary maintenance. Take it slow and easy. You cannot help any lost fry back to their parents and they will probably die on their own.

I feed my fry five times each day. I always remove any uneaten food within one hour. (Since I am retired, my time is my own and I can be this attentive to my fish.)

You will find that young discus (should) eat all the time and are always looking for food. Small, frequent feedings are much more desirable than large feeds between long fasts. Discus have very small stomachs. They pass food through very quickly and need to eat as often as possible.

### Moving the Fry

When the fry are about 10 to 15 days old, it's time for them to be moved to their own rearing tank. They will have grown to about four times their hatchling size and are mature enough to survive on their own. A 20-gallon tank is a perfect size for these youngsters. A mature sponge filter will take care of their water quality and set the heater at 86°F. Feed the babies newly hatched brine shrimp as often as ten times per day. When they are the size of a dime you can start to train them on crushed or powdered flake foods. Within six weeks to two months, the fry will be about one inch in length and then can be reared on finely ground versions of your adult discus feed.

### Artificial Hatching and Rearing

Personally I do not favor the removal of discus eggs from the parent discus. I feel the adults should be allowed to tend their fry, and the fry should be allowed to feed from the skin of the parents. I have hatched and reared discus both ways, and have found that in the long run it's just not worth the time or effort. There are many breeders who swear by artificial hatching and rearing as a means to get the most fry possible, but I feel that it's rushing things a bit to have the pair back in the production line right after spawning. It is true that once you have your system down pat and can operate exactly the same way with each spawn that you can save more fry. However, I find that the work involved far outweighs any advantage in increased fry production.

The method used to hatch out the eggs is about the same as for angelfish eggs. Remove the spawning cone from the tank (Keep the eggs covered with water at all times!) and place them in a container with identical water conditions. Add methylene blue or acriflavin to prevent fungus. Add an airstone positioned so the bubbles are close to but not hitting the eggs and keep water at 86 degrees. When the eggs hatch out and the fry become free-swimming, remove them with a suction baster to a shallow plastic bowl no more the four inches deep. Before adding the fry, spread a light film of powdered baker's egg yolk around the edge of the bowl. Work a little water into the egg yolk to make a paste. Use only very small amounts as needed. You should add spirulina algae powder to the mix this will increase growth through-out the entire life span of the fish. I have always added royal jelly bee mix to the egg yolk mixture. Do not add any

vitamins to the mixture. Let the egg set for a while and add water to the bowl to just above the bottom of the egg yolk. You must change the water often to keep from fouling the water with uneaten egg yolk. The fry must be fed every four to six hours and moved to a new bowl with clean water in between. The water in the bowls must be identical in pH and temperature at each change. After about five or six days you can start feeding baby brine shrimp mixed into the mixture and on the seventh or eighth day live baby brine can be fed. After that time you can rear them as regular fry. If you use this method, remember that any soap on your hands or the equipment will kill the fry...be careful and good luck.

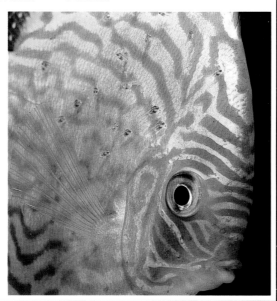

The parents will be very suspicious of anyone who goes near the tank when they are leading fry. Give them a break. Don't bring every visitor to look at the youngsters.

# Discus Health and Treatments

From time to time every discus keeper will have to deal with fish diseases. If you are following the proper procedures concerning water quality, feeding, and quarantine of new discus, this should be a rare occurrence—but it will happen. The main point to remember is do not panic! Panic will lead to costly mistakes. When disease shows up, it's time for cool judgment. There are many books that cover disease and treatment of tropical fishes, even some specifically aimed at discus diseases. You should be familiar with the contents of these books *before* you have to contend with any sick fish. One excellent example is T.F.H. publication TS-169, *Discus Health* by Dieter Untergasser.

There are many, many diseases that can attack fishes. Some, like "the new discus disease," are still a mystery even to the experts. The best most aquarists can do is give our discus the best possible care we can and hope that when a disease does occur that it is something that we will be equipped to deal with.

Some of us will have microscopes and other diagnostic tools at our disposal. For those with the background, the skill, and the interest in microbiology, by all means use your microscopes to identify disease-causing organisms and apply scientific methods to treat and hopefully cure your sick fishes. Then, publish your findings in magazines like *Tropical Fish Hobbyist* so we can all share the wealth.

**THE PROTECTIVE SLIME COAT**

Your health-care regimen starts with your water quality. I cannot repeat myself often enough. The water that discus are kept in has a tremendous impact on their ability to ward off the ever-present disease organisms that are waiting, dormant, for a weakened fish so they can gain a foothold.

Discus are designed by nature to live in certain, specific water conditions.

They can survive in water of differing values, but their natural resistance to disease will be reduced. The slime coat that protects the skin and feeds the fry of the discus is produced most efficiently in soft, acid water. A discus that has a healthy slime coat and healthy skin is more ably defended against the organisms that attack the skin. Some of these organisms include: gill and skin flukes (trematodes); gill and skin flagellates (*Costia, Cryptobia,* and *Oodinium*); parasites (*Ichthyophthirius, Chilodonella, Tetrahymena, Trichodina*); bacteria; and fungi.

## THE QUALITY OF WATER

The water quality and chemistry are not important only in the production of the slime coat, but there is a very strong relationship between water chemistry and stress

One of the saddest sights to a discus keeper. Remove the sick fish to a hospital tank so all the fish don't become afflicted.

(or lack of it). Discus, like any other living being, have a finite capacity for enduring stress. The vital energy required for the body to function normally under inappropriate water conditions adds an unnecessary stress factor to otherwise healthy discus. This is especially true with respect to adjustments of pH.

When you are reducing the pH of your water remember that a 1-unit drop from 7 to 6.9 represents a 10-fold concentration in acids and a further drop from 6 to 5 has increased acidity 100 times! Rapid increases in the acidity of your water will cause your fish to develop a slimy, whitish coat and pieces of skin will start to flake off—acid burns. This is a serious condition and a totally preventable one! To correct this problem, slowly change the water in the tank until the pH is again at an acceptable level.

### Chlorine

Chlorine is added into our water supplies to ensure that the water from our taps is safe to drink. Unfortunately, our discus will not be drinking this chlorinated water, but breathing it and with very harmful results.

Chlorine burns the gills! A fish with chlorine poisoning has great difficulty breathing and will die with repeated doses of untreated chlorinated tap water.

Your nose will tell you if your water has been treated with chlorine. (Usually it has been.) The water will smell faintly of household bleach...or a swimming pool! Aeration forces the chlorine gas out of the water. If you are using reverse osmosis, chlorine is removed by the process. Aging the water will remove chlorine. There are even chlorine removers that you can buy at your pet shop. Any one of these precautions will safeguard the health of your discus' gills.

Chloramine, unfortunately, is not so simply dealt with. Some municipalities are now using chlorine *and* ammonia, chloramine, to purify the water supply. There are very simple test kits that will tell the story. Chloramine must be removed from any water that is to be used for discus. A chloramine remover is available at your pet shop. Use it in appropriate doses to remove chloramine whenever you are adding water to your aquarium.

## Ammonia, Nitrite, and Nitrate Poisoning

Ammonia and nitrite poisoning are the result of poor water changing habits, overfeeding, and bad filtration. The symptoms start with tiny white dots covering the skin and advance to include pale fins that fray and fall off, increased skin mucous production, gill damage, and damage to the internal organs leading to death.

The presence of ammonia, nitrite, and nitrates in your water can be totally eliminated by biological filtration, water changes, and careful feeding. While nitrate, the end-product of biological filtration, has long been considered harmless to fishes, this is not entirely true and should only be thought of as "less harmful" than ammonia and nitrite. Nitrates are easily removed from the aquarium. Change some of that water.

## INJURIES

Accidents will happen. There will be times when your fish will be injured in the normal course of their daily lives. Perhaps a tankmate has gotten a bit too rough or maybe the fish has taken a fright and dashed itself against some object (previously thought to be safe) in the tank. Scratches, missing scales, and even cuts are not rare in the aquarium. These wounds should be treated quickly before infection or fungus invade the tissue.

Fin and tail rot is bacterial in origin and can be prevented with good water quality.

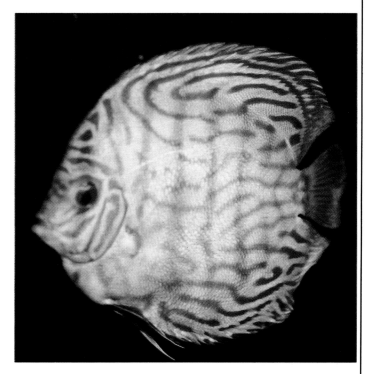

Remove the damaged fish to a small quarantine tank where the extent of the injury can be observed. Methylene blue is an excellent prophylactic medication against fungus and bacterial invasion of small wounds such as scratches and lacerations.

Use five teaspoons for three gallons of water. N.B. All medications should be used according to label instructions. Manufacturers often differ in their dilutions of the packaged product. Methylene blue should not be used in the presence of biological filtration—it will destroy the desirable bacteria along with the disease-causing organisms. Hence the necessity of treating the injured fish in a small hospital tank. Feed lightly or not at all in the confines of this small tank. Change the water, decreasing the amount of methylene blue until the wound is healed. Caution: Methylene blue is a strong dye and will stain everything it contacts. Methylene blue is a strong medication and should not be used for more than three days. The fish under treatment should also be carefully monitored while in the methylene blue bath.

**THE IMPORTANCE OF DIET**

We don't even have to think about variety in our own diets. We automatically choose to eat different foods because a diet of all steak would be just as boring and unhealthy as a diet that consisted solely of cookies and soda. The same is true for our discus. Our discus depend on us for every bite they eat and if we want to keep them in good health and condition, the right kind of variety is essential. Train your discus to eat many different kinds of foods and supplement these foods with the proper vitamins and you will avoid the nutritional deficiencies that will ruin their natural good health.

Aside from variety, however, there are other feeding habits that will affect the health of our discus. Of course we avoid any live foods that can carry parasites and diseases, but what about spoiled foods? Old and badly stored prepared foods are hazardous. Fungi, bacteria, and molds multiply rapidly in food containers kept in the humid conditions of most fishrooms. Buy only as much prepared food as you will use in a month and keep it in a dry place.

Frozen foods can be unfit for fish consumption. If the food has thawed and been refrozen, there is a good chance that it is spoiled. If the food is gray—and it shouldn't be—throw it out. Fishes can get food poisoning. Frozen foods should be thawed before being fed to your discus. A large piece of frozen beefheart will cause more than an upset stomach in an aggressively feeding discus.

### SIGNS AND SYMPTOMS

Careful observation of your fish on a regular basis will help you to detect signs of ill health before the condition has reached a critical stage. Watch your fish when you feed them. This is most revealing. You will usually be able to get a good look at every fish from every angle. Be suspicious if you see that a fish is not eating. Loss of appetite is a symptom, especially in a fish that had previously had good appetite. Check the fish's attitude. Lethargy is a sign of illness, so is flightiness. Erratic swimming and loss of balance point to trouble. (Discus do swim oddly at times. If you know your fish you will be able to tell what is normal and what is not.) Is the skin healthy? Sliminess, skin spots, fin erosion, white patches on

the skin, darkening of the body—all are symptoms.

Rapid breathing is another symptom. Discus will hyperventilate when they are excited by food or being chased or otherwise stressed, but when a quiet fish has gill beats in excess of one per second, it could be in trouble. If the nitrate level is okay and there is enough oxygen in the water, there is a possibility of gill disease or flukes.

There are, of course, many other symptoms that can manifest themselves in

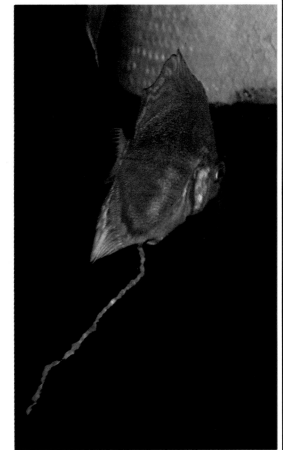

Stringy white feces are a sign of intestinal parasites. Treat fish accordingly.

sick discus. These are but a few of the alarm bells that should send an aquarist to his water test kit and discus reference books.

## DIAGNOSIS AND TREATMENTS

The diseases you can see are usually the easiest to diagnose and treat properly. If a fish is showing external symptoms, it is usually easier to make your diagnosis through the process of elimination and comparison with published photos of other fishes with the same condition. Even so, many times misdiagnoses are made and the fish is treated for a totally unrelated condition. Sometimes the fish recovers in spite of the treatment it has received rather than because of it.

Internal conditions are naturally much more difficult to diagnose. The symptoms of many intestinal conditions are similar and without professional equipment and training, often an educated guess is the closest an aquarist can come to a diagnosis.

Before any treatment is attempted, you should fully understand the nature of the disease you are trying to treat and any side-effects a given chemical may produce in your discus both for the short and long term. There is not much point in controlling a disease if the treatment kills the fish or render it useless as a breeder later in life. Furthermore, medications should not be used as prophylaxis. This will only strengthen the pathogens and weaken the fishes. If you think you can use small doses of, say, an anti-ich medication to prevent ich, you are kidding yourself and placing your discus in grave danger. All medications, even the most common, are powerful drugs and should be used only in the proper dosages for the recommended duration of treatment.

### Bacterial Tail and Fin Rot

Bacterial infections, like fin and tail rot, are not confined to discus but are found in all freshwater fishes. The affected fish display one or more of the following symptoms: fin degeneration, gill degeneration, inflammation of the mouth, and yellow mucous around the affected areas. One sign that the condition is truly bacterial is that the fins drop off, but the fin rays remain.

These bacteria are

present in all warm waters, but increase when the organic load is high in the aquarium. Acriflavine is an effective therapy used according to manufacturer's directions. The antibiotic, neomycin sulfate, can be used as a last resort.

## Saprolegnia

Saprolegnia, or fungus, is found in all aquatic environments. They are normally occupied with the break-down of waste in aquarium. Again, with clean water and siphoning of food remains, the fish are generally safe from fungus unless the skin has been damaged in some way. The fungi spores settle into the wound and germinate into a cottony mass like we sometimes see on an overlooked piece of beefheart that has been floating around in the aquarium. Once the fungus has settled into the skin it grows outward as we can see, but the danger is two-fold. The fungus devours the tissue inwardly as well and as it grows and reproduces, produces toxic materials that poison the fish. While treatment is not

difficult, the speed with which you act can mean the difference between life and death for a fish with a fungal infection.

If saprolegnia is suspected, it is imperative that the fish be moved to a quarantine tank treated with an appropriate dose of

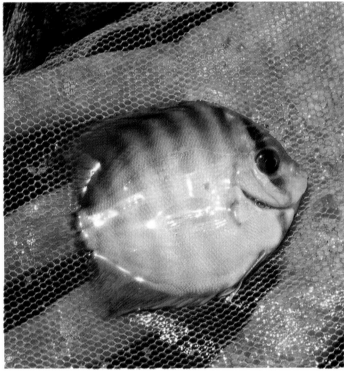

Fish with short gill covers are culls. Do not sell them or allow them to reproduce.

methylene blue. Nystatin should be used to treat the wound itself.

## Ichthyophthirius

Ich, as the infestation with the parasite *Ichthyophthirius multifilis* is commonly known, is no stranger to fishkeepers, but is not a common disease of discus. Ich is not usually a problem in the warm waters preferred by discus, but chilling of the fish will lower its resistance to the parasites and any new fish is at risk as well.

The symptoms of ich infestation are small white spots on the skin, thickened mucous membrane, and skin discoloration, with the affected fish rubbing its body on objects in the tank as if it were scratching an itch. Early stages of ich can usually be treated quite well with malachite green per manufacturer's instructions and the elevation of the water temperature to 90°F for two weeks. This interrupts the life cycle of the parasites. Severe ich can be life-threatening, so do not ignore a fish that is rubbing itself on objects in the aquarium, even if you don't yet notice other symptoms.

### Medicated Baths

Most treatable skin diseases are caused by bacteria, parasites, or fungus and if caught in time, will respond well to treatment with one of the dyes like malachite green or methylene blue. Again, even though these medications are thought to be safe because they are easy to obtain, they are strong chemicals and should be used with care. *All medications should be kept well out of reach of children!* Malachite green in particular is a powerful toxin and overdoses are very dangerous to fishes. It is better to use short baths in small doses rather than expect the medication to work like a bomb. It is also more toxic in the soft, acid water preferred by discus than neutral water conditions and the dosage should be carefully calculated with this in mind. Warning: Malachite green is irritating to the skin, poisonous if swallowed, and possibly carcinogenic. If you feel ill after working with malachite green, consult your doctor immediately.

### Intestinal Parasites

Worms are a fact of life for fishes. Every fish carries its own complement of intestinal worms. When the fish is in good health, these worms are not a problem, but as soon as the fish's natural immunity is compromised, the populations increase and compound the health problems of the already weakened fish.

Hairworms (*Capillaria*) are nematodes that are always present in the intestine, but can get out of control when large numbers of eggs are introduced with live foods, the fish is stressed, or when new fish are introduced to the community. A fish with an overgrowth of hairworms will turn dark and lose its appetite. Flubendazol is the treatment of choice for hairworms. Flubendazol therapy is often used during the quarantine period to "clean out" new fish and ensure they are not carrying into the community.

## Tapeworms

Tapeworms are common in discus and can accumulate in large numbers in the intestines of discus. A tapeworm infestation usually shows up with symptoms of constipation and malnutrition. Often, the first indication you will have that your fish is infested with tapeworms is when you see a long, white worm hanging from the vent of the fish or floating in the tank. You will try to convince yourself that this is a piece of white thread, or a loose piece of silicone from the tank. You are probably wrong. Flubendazol or Droncit will take care of this little

problem. We worm our dogs and cats every year. Why do people think that fish shouldn't also be wormed?

## Parasitic Flagellates

Intestinal parasites cannot multiply readily in healthy fish, but stresses, such as transport, can cause massive population explosions of these pesky parasites. A discus with intestinal parasite problems will have long, white feces, refuse food, become emaciated, and look very sick. Metronidazole is very effective against most species of flagellate when used according to directions. Metronidazole treatment should be

Emaciated, stunted, and diseased. What *not* to look for when buying discus.

repeated after about five days to nip the next generation of flagellates in the bud.

**Costia**

*Costia* are skin flagellates that multiply quickly on weakened fishes. Shipping stress is notorious for bringing out the *Costia* in otherwise healthy discus. Many new discus owners open their shipping boxes and are dismayed to find their fish in terrible shape with missing patches of skin with reddened margins and hemorrhage. The breeder who shipped the fish is not necessarily to blame! It happens.

There are several treatments for *Costia*. Malachite green and trypaflavine works, as does formalin. A bath of common table salt in water works as well. For a salt bath, mix 1 level teaspoon of kosher salt per gallon of water. Keep the fish in the bath for 10 to 20 minutes a day until the skin is cleared. Make a new batch for every treatment.

**Oodinium**

Velvet, or *Oodinium*, is usually not too much of a problem in the discus aquarium. The flagellates do not do well in water over 86°F. A fish with velvet looks like it has been

dusted with talcum; there are tiny white dots all over the body. If the fish is seriously infested, the skin will start to come off in pieces. Copper sulfate used strictly according to manufacturer's directions is an effective treatment.

**Flukes**

Flukes (trematodes) are parasites that live on the gills or skin of fishes. Microscopic examination is required for exact diagnosis of the different flukes, but generally the skin flukes, *Gyrodactylus*, cause the afflicted fish to rub themselves, exude bluish mucus, and have blotchy looking skin. Flubendazol is effective. Masoten is also used. Gill flukes, *Dactylogyrus*, cause the infested fish to gasp at the water's surface with gills wide open while they suffocate. Flubenol 5% is the therapy.

Fortunately, discus usually acquire an immunity to flukes by the age of four to six months. Discus usually pick up the fluke eggs right from their parents when they are feeding from their slime. The adult fish are past the age where the flukes will affect them, but it happens that the young, crowded juveniles are seriously afflicted, stop growing, and begin to show signs of infestation.

## Hole-in-the-Head Disease

The holes we often see in the heads of discus and other large cichlids are not caused by any external pathogen, but are rather a sign of a nutritional deficiency, most particularly a lack of vitamin D. The diet is often, but not always, lacking in vitamin D, calcium, and phosphorus. The problem could stem from flagellates in the intestine that interfere with the fish's absorption of its food.

Hole-in-the-head can be corrected by adding a multivitamin that contains these elements to the diet. The holes will close over in a few weeks once the supplements have been added to the diet.

Hole-in-the-head symptoms could lead one to believe that the fish has worms coming out of its head. This is pus. As the pus comes out of the smaller holes, it does not immediately detach from the wound and "wiggles" on the head. The pus will fall off and (if your tank has no substrate) leave a small white smear on the glass.

## Treatment for Wild Fish

When wild discus arrive, they are usually well infested with any number of parasites, worms. . .what have you. They must be cleaned up before they are introduced to their permanent aquarium, and certainly before they are introduced to any of your stock! This is my method for cleaning up new stock before I start taming or conditioning them for breeding. There are other methods that work equally well but this is my way of doing it.

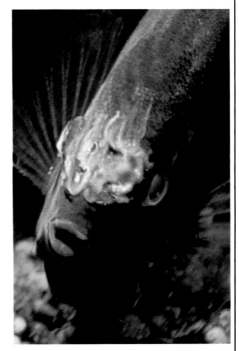

Hole-in-the-head can be quite severe at times. Keep your water quality good.

When the fish arrive, they need two things above all else: rest and relief from stress and medical treatment for parasites and shipping injuries. They also are half starved and need high-quality food. I place the fish in a 100-gallon tank. (About ten fish to a tank is a good stocking level.) There is a lot of deep cover in this tank. I make lots of private places using dark plastic trash bags cut into

1 1/2-inch strips, tied together, weighted, and placed on the bottom of the tank. These plastic strips are magic! The fish feel very secure and calm down very quickly when I use them in the tank. They don't get in the way when I clean the tank; they just float aside.

threatening conditions are found, the light is again dimmed and the fish are allowed to rest in quiet for up to two weeks. During this time  they are fed only live food, mostly blackworms. The fish are checked each day for any sign of fin-rot or ich.

After about ten days to two weeks the fish are moved to 20-gallon tanks (four fish per tank.) If the fish are in generally strong with no open cuts or sores, I treat them for external parasites with a ten-minute bath in potassium permanganate and salt. I mix one teaspoon of potassium permanganate and two teaspoons of common salt in warm water and add slowly to the 20-gallon tanks over    five-minute's time. The fish are removed after exactly ten minutes to clean aged water. I then adjust the ph to 5.8 and temperature is set at 86°F.

Swim bladder problems are very sad to see in discus, but many times the fish will spawn and raise its babies even though it can't swim straight.

They are removed a few at a time as the fish get more used to their new home.

The water in this tank is well aged and filtered with peat. I do not worry about the pH at this time. The lighting is very dim. I brighten the light only to check on physical condition of the new arrivals. I look for cuts or skin injuries, fin-rot, ich, etc. If no life-

From this point on, the discus are trained to eat only beefheart and flake food. They are never again given blackworms. In the beefheart I mix a product

called Worm-out and metronidazole. These products will kill most of the internal parasites and reduce tapeworms to manageable levels.

Once these treatments have been carried out, you can move the discus to 50-gallon tanks and start hand taming the fish and developing that bond of trust that is required before spawning can occur.

The above treatment can be used with all newly arriving discus but is an absolute requirement when you bring wild discus into your fishroom.

# Advice and Afterthoughts

I have been in the fish business for well over thirty years and have found that a lot of problems can be avoided. You can have better results in your efforts to spawn discus and the number one way to do this is clean...extra clean water at all times.

Keep stress on your fish low at all times.

Once you have found a spawning pair, do not move them around from tank to tank. They should be allowed their own tank for life.

Treat sick fish quickly. Do not mix new fish with your older stock. When new fish are bought, treat them as if they were carrying a deadly disease for the first 30 to 45 days after arrival. They just might be!!!

If a pair of fish is reluctant to spawn and you know they should, put a divider between them for a few days until they can't wait to get back together.

Using peat filtered water will help you keep the pH range required.

Buying good starter stock is another important point to remember. Your investment at the start will pay you back many times, especially when you consider the amount of tender loving care you will give these fish.

Proper feeding at regular times!

I recommend that each tank be assigned it's own net. I never use the same net in different tanks. Nets are cheap, discus are not.

Common filtration systems should be avoided. Each tank and each pair should have it's own filter with no mixing of water or filters.

Keep traffic in your fish room as low as possible. Do not allow strangers near your spawning tanks.

Keep your lighting subdued.

Move slowly when working around your tanks; discus are frightened by quick movements.

to turn them on, try this. Set the temperature at 86°F. Adjust your pH to 5.8. Drain one-half of the water. Replace with cold tap water. Do not adjust the temperature, but let it come back to 86°F. Adjust

Now I am going to reveal the real secret to spawning discus. Are you ready? Patience. Without it, don't even think about keeping discus.

When you have a pair that will not spawn—you know they are a good pair, but you just cannot seem

the pH back to 5.8, and drop the water temperature to 82°F. Nine times out of ten they will spawn within 24 hours. That one time out of ten when they won't, place a clear glass divider between the male and female so they can see each other but not touch. Feed

If you want plants, be sure they can live in discus water.

This is a brown discus. Yes, it is. It just happens to carry a lot of blue.

Wild green discus, *Symphysodon aequifasciatus aequifasciatus*.

More brown discus. As you can see, the names of discus do not always match up with their colors. This is often frustrating and confusing.

them well to condition for spawning and remove the divider after two weeks. They should get down to work and spawn quickly. This enforced separation added to the above water change should never fail. Another method is to place the clear glass divider in tank as before, but this

Build a wire cover that you can slip over the spawning cone or surface, so they can still see and fan their eggs but cannot reach them. This egg-guard can be made out of rabbit wire. One-quarter inch square holes will allow fanning, but not eating of the eggs. In most cases, once the

time place a third fish behind it. That will cause the male fish to defend the spawning area. After about three or four days, remove the third fish and the glass divider.

Young spawning discus tend to eat their eggs until they are older and more into parenting. If you want to save the eggs, try this.

eggs hatch into wrigglers, the parents will not eat the fry.

When setting up new tanks for newly paired breeders, save water you remove with normal water changes from a tank that has a good spawning pair. Place this water in your new tank. Run a second sponge filter in the tank

Success with discus! A pair of beautiful cobalts are tending their large spawn.

with the spawning pair for about two weeks, then add this filter to the new tank. You will find this goes a long way towards getting new pairs active in the spawning sense.

Never use tap water to clean sponge filters from tanks containing a good spawning pair. Use aged old water. Do not kill the bacteria in your sponge with tap water. If you do, the pair will most likely stop spawning for a while.

If you have shy or frightened discus add guppies to the tank for a week or so. They will calm your discus and should your discus stop eating this will cause them to start feeding again. (Use adult guppies.)

A trusting bond and handfeeding of discus requires a lot of time and

Red turquoise showing excellent color of body and eye.

**Left:** This is a striking fish! It is called a red turquoise, but see what the light does to the color. **Below:** What's that discus doing in there with the angelfish?

Royal blue wild-caught discus.

effort but makes for a much more enjoyable and rewarding experience with discus.

Never, never, ever keep angelfish with discus. Never, never.

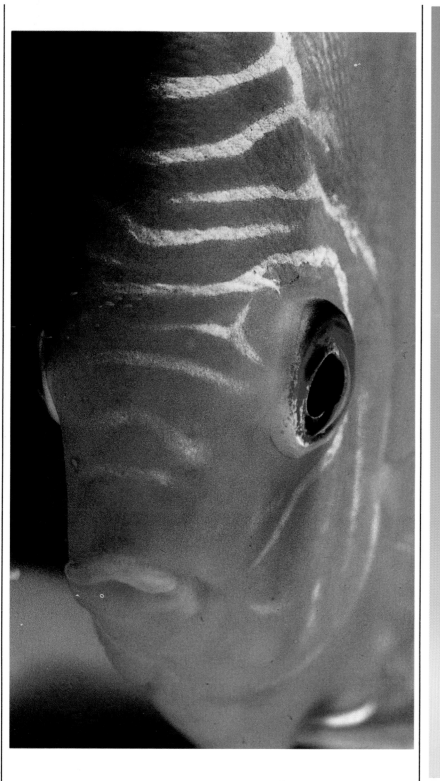

A portrait of the "King of the Aquarium."

# Index

**Bold type** indicates a photo or illustration.